Beautiful Summer!
For Kids

Nature Books for Kids
By K. Bennett
Mendon Cottage Books

JD-Biz Publishing

Read Some Amazing Animal Books

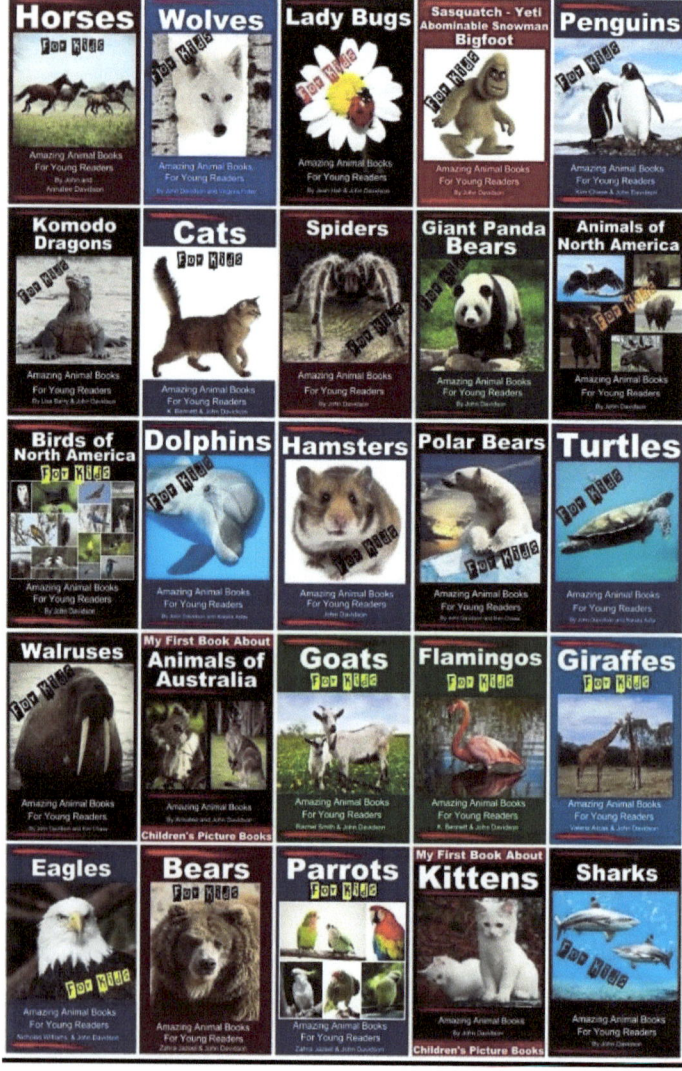

Purchase at Amazon.com

Table of Contents

Introduction

Yellow butterflies look like flowers flying through the warm summer air. ~ Andrea Willis

Summer: Summer is a wonderful season with long days and lots of warm sunlight!

In the Northern Hemisphere this season happens in June, July, and August. But in the Southern Hemisphere this season happens in December, January, and February.

Does this sound a bit confusing?

Don't worry. We will explain what it all means in this book and how exciting summer can be!

What do you like about Summer?

Many kids love to do fun things outdoors. Others might like to do fun things indoors. What about you? What do you like best? Outside or Inside?

Summer is also exciting for many school children. Can you guess why? Did you guess **Summer vacation**? Yes! This can be a very fun time for lots of young ones!

What else happens in Summer?

Did you think of playing games like volleyball? Or maybe swimming in a nice pool or in the sea? What about outdoor picnics?

When you think about these fun things you might like Summer best! But let's find out what is so special about this season.

As we said before, Summer starts during the month of June in the Northern Hemisphere. It happens around the 20th – 22nd of the month.

We get this season because the earth tilts towards the sun. And when this happens, we have the LONGEST day in the year. This is called the Summer Solstice and it is pretty amazing! Why?

Because when it is the longest day for you, it is the SHORTEST day on earth for someone else! How is that possible?

The seasons come from the way the earth goes around the sun. As the earth travels, different parts of the planet get different amounts of sunlight.

The earth also spins around in a circle and this happens every 24 hours. This is called a day. While the earth spins it doesn't stand straight up. It bends or tilts and this is where we get the seasons!

Let's see how this works…

This about it like this... When one part of the earth is tilted or bends towards the sun, the other part is tilted or bends away from the sun.

So…one end is SUMMER and the other end is WINTER.

For those who have summer, it is the longest day but for those who have winter it is the shortest day.

What do you think about this fact?

TEST YOUR SKILLS

On December 21st…

People who live in the Northern Hemisphere have a Winter Solstice. How is that different than a Summer solstice or is it the same? To help you in your search remember that Solstice comes from a Latin term that means: Sun stationary. This means the sun seems to stand still!

Don't forget to ask for permission before you search online.

How is summer different?

Summer is a great season for lots of reasons and one of the biggest is called: **Summer vacation**. We talked about it just a little before. You might enjoy doing fun things after school but do you know why you get summer vacation? Where the idea comes from? Here is a bit of history for you!

*Horace Mann lived during the 1800's and in the year 1840 he decided school children needed a break from studying too long. Why? He said if you worked school children too hard, they could get stressed and that would hurt their minds and bodies. His words and hard work helped to give children a break from school during summer.

There are a ton of activities you can do in summertime like…

-Eat a nice, tasty picnic at the park or in your backyard. Use lots of colored balloons to make it even more fun! You could try inflatable pools and have a pool party and picnic together.

-Build a pretty sandcastle and decorate it with colorful seashells.

-Try roasted hotdogs on sticks. Yum! Yum!

-Ride your bicycle on a nice, clean trail. (Do not ride alone! Get your parents or an adult to go along with you.)

-Find a nice creek and watch the ducks wade by or feed them with some nice breadcrumbs.

-Go swimming on a pretty beach!

-Instead of planting a flower garden, plant a butterfly garden. If you don't know how, I will tell you later on in this book. It might be fun so give it a try!

-Dress up like a pirate and build a fort on the beach or in your backyard.

-Visit a museum to find out about an old civilization you didn't know anything about!

-Make interesting sand art.

-Make a large drawing project and get your friends to help you. Then hang it on the wall. Nice job!

-Get a map of the United States or the World and decide where you might like to visit or explore.

-Try your hand at making homemade pizza. Try different toppings and flavors. Do not forget to get an adult's permission before you start!

Do you like these ideas? Great! There are many more fun activities to do during summer. Log on to the Care.com website and search for "101 fun things to do with Kids during summer." or click the link below:

https://www.care.com/a/101-fun-things-to-do-with-kids-this-summer-1305030150

Have fun!

Chapter 1

Learning is fun!

What happens to plants in Summer time?

Summer can be a great time for plants or it can be a bad time if the sun is too hot! But for most plants, summer is very important. Do you remember why sunlight is so important to plants?

Plants need the warm sun to grow well and during summer the sun is nice and strong. Sunlight is not only important for energy but also for food. After all, plants need to eat too!

What kind of food do plants eat? Did you guess a hamburger? No? What about a nice ham sandwich? No? A tasty salad? No? Then what do plants eat?

Keep on guessing….

Before we answer, let me ask you… why do you eat food? You might say: I eat to live! Well, plants feel the same way. They eat to live. But their food is a lot different than your food. For one thing, plants can make their own food to eat! So you don't have to cook for them. What a smart plant!

To make their own food, plants need 3 things.

-Sunlight

-Water

-Carbon Dioxide

When plants get these three things they turn it into something called: GLUCOSE. And this is what the plants eat and store to get energy. Then we can eat the delicious fruit that come from the plants. So plants really "cook" for us!

Many plants love summer. Let's learn about three of them.

Hydrangeas!

Hydrangeas are beautiful flowers that look like big snowballs on a stem! These flowers grow in bunches and come from Southern and Eastern Asia. Some are blue, pink, red and purple but most of the species are a beautiful white color. The color of the flower depends on what kind of soil it grows in. Isn't that amazing?

These flowers have very interesting names like…

-Mophead

-Panicle

-Lacecap

Hydrangeas love summer so much they are called: Endless summer!

Snow in Summer!

Did you know there is a flower species called Snow in Summer? Can you guess what color it is? Did you say white? Good job! These flowers are very pretty and when they bloom, they look like snow.

They love the summer sun and grow quickly. This plant is also called: Cerastium Silver Carpet. This is because the white looks a little like silver and when it covers the ground, it looks like a beautiful carpet!

African Marigolds!

African Marigolds are beautiful and bright flowers that grow on a long stem. They can grow 3 feet high and bloom five inch flowering balls! Some of these species can be small but many of them are tall.

The summer sun is good for the African Marigolds and they grow nice and tall. There are four species of Marigolds.

-African
-French
-Triploid
-Single

Each one of these amazing plants is different but they are all beautiful! Which one do you like best?

Source: (www.gardeningknowhow.com & www.Ehow.com)

Don't forget…

Plants have roots and the roots go deep into the ground. So…. if water stays on the top of the soil for a long time, will the roots of the plant get the water it needs?

Another important step to remember is to water your plants the right way. If you give it too little your little plant will die and if you give it too much, your little plant will drown.

So be careful and measure the water you pour on your plants. Your parents can help you or you can research online. Don't forget to get permission before you do!

Chapter 2

Nature is amazing!

More changes happen during summertime in the animal kingdom.
Let's learn about five of them and what they do in the hot summer
days!

(Source: www.Care2.com)

Bumblebees:

The queen bee hibernates to survive the winter and she hides herself
from the world until it gets warmer. Summer is the perfect time for
her to wake up and start a new colony with lots of worker bees.
These workers love the sunlight and they work very hard in the warm

months pollinating the flowers and making delicious honey. Yum! Yum!

Hedgehogs:

These cute like spiky animals sleep like a baby during the winter. When the spring and summer months come, hedgehogs come out to play! But they don't like the daylight too much and prefer to run around at night.

Hedgehogs are great at pest control! They will eat lots of insects, snails, worms and other little garden creatures. During the warm summer months, Hedgehogs grow a family of hoglets (baby hedgehogs) and usually have 4 or 5 little ones in a litter.

Box Turtles:

These amazing turtles can live for over 100 years! They don't really like the cold and hibernate during winter. When summer comes around they wake up to enjoy the warm sunlight.

Sometime it gets a little too hot during summer so box turtles like the early morning and after the rain. And if it gets much hotter, they find a nice pool of water with shade to cool off! Or they might dig a burrow into the mud or an old rotten log and relax for a while. How do you cool off?

Moths:

Moths are part of the butterfly family. They are very active during summer and love warm days. They are wonderful at pollinating plants and if we had no months, lots of tasty food would disappear! Distractify.com calls moths: "The night shift of the Earth's pollination industry." When butterflies and bees go home for the night, can you guess what moths are doing? Yes! They are busy working their little wings off to pollinate flowers. Good job little moth!

Badgers:

Badgers have a lot of fun during the summer months. They live underground in tunnels with a large group of other badgers and are very social animals. During winter they hibernate but when summer comes around, they are ready to play! And the warm summer evenings when the sun goes down is a perfect time for badgers.

How about you? Do you like to play with your friends in the morning or evening?

FUN FACTS FOR KIDS:

Do you remember the names of ALL the seasons? Read here to refresh your memory!

-Spring

-Summer

-Fall (Autumn)

-Winter!

Which season do you like more? Did you think of spring or summer? Or did you pick fall or winter? Is there a reason you like one more than the other? Think about your reasons, write them down or share with others!

There are lots of fun summertime activities and a **Scavenger Hunt** is a fun activity you might like to try. Have you ever played this game before? If not, here are some great ideas adapted from **Scavenger-hunt.org** to help you.

First: Form a team or group. Then pick a topic for your hunt. You might choose a special day of the year or you might choose a theme you want to learn more about. For example, you might want to learn more about cats, dogs, birds, or just nature in general. Whatever theme you choose, just remember to have fun!

Type: Now that you have your players and theme, let's decide on the type of hunt you would like to do. You may choose an item each player has to find. Or you might choose a photo each player needs to take or a small video or just write down an interesting note.

Item: If you choose an item, each player should collect that item. For example, if you tell players they need to collect a round leaf, then the player will look for a round leaf and bring it back to the group. Or you might decide to have your players collect 5 different types of leaves in different colors. The choice is up to you!

If you choose to ask for a photo, your players must take a picture of the items on the list. Please be careful and ONLY take pictures you are allowed to take! Do not get in trouble for snapping the wrong thing.

Location: Pick a nice place to do the hunt. It might be on the beach, in a park or at the zoo. There are many other great locations to choose from and you may have ideas of your own. You can also get a parent or a guardian to help you.

List: You will need a list for the hunt with the items each player must find.

Time: Timing is very important. There is a time for the hunt to begin and there is a time for the hunt to end.

Rules: Set your rules. This is what players can and cannot do and then…

Get started!

Note: Don't forget to have a prize for the winner and a treat for the other teams. There is no reason why there should be only ONE winner for the hunt. Share with everyone as a team and have a great time!

Chapter 3

I hope you enjoyed this book on Beautiful Summer! Here are just a few more facts you may like to know.

- Lots of people go on holiday during summer vacation and children love it too. One of the best places to go during summer is to the beach. Other places that are nice are Maui, Fiji, Nice and Mykonos, which are all beautiful places to visit. Have you ever been there?

- The month of June gets its name from the Romans. A goddess named Juno, which is the wife of Jupiter.

-The month of July comes from a Roman ruler by the name of Julius Caesar.

-The month of August gets its name from another Roman ruler by the name of Caesar Augustus.

- In the United States more people buy ice cream during the month of July!

-The North American Butterfly Association (NABA) counts the butterflies in the United States, Mexico and Canada during summer in the month of July. In 2014, they had over 400 different counting stations. That's a lot of counting!

-During the summer something very interesting happens to the Eiffel tower in France. Did you know the tower grows? Why? The tower is made out of metal, and iron. When this material gets very hot it expands, and gets a little longer. Summer is very hot so this tower expands or stretches up to 6 inches!

KEEP LEARNING!

Spring is one of the four seasons. And the reason why we have seasons is because of the earth's tilt towards the sun as we said in the beginning. Do you remember how many degrees it is tilted? Can you guess?

1- $14.76°$ (Fourteen point seventy-six degrees)

2- $20.22°$ (Twenty point twenty-two degrees)

3- $23.45°$ (Twenty-three point forty-five degrees)

If you chose number 3 you are correct! This is what gives the earth the beautiful seasons during the year.

Vocabulary:

During the summer season you will hear many different words that people use. Words like:

-Blistering heat

-Road trip

-Stifling

-Summer solstice

-Muggy

-Swim fins

-Sweltering

-Searing heat

-Boating

-Popsicle

-Recreation

-Outings

-Journey

-Hiking

-Canoeing

-Sandcastle

-Humidity

-Trunks (Hint: It does not refer to a tree)

-Tan

-Frisbee

Do you know what any of these words mean? If you are not sure, ask your parent or a guardian's permission to search for the definition. I hope you learn something new!

(*www.dictionary.com*)

Conclusion:

In conclusion: Summer, like each of the four seasons, is unique and does wonderful things for our planet. Here are a few more ideas to help you learn more about this amazing season!

More Ideas!

Why don't you research how some animals behave during this season? Here are some animals that do interesting things during summertime.

-Canadian Grizzly Bear. (For some reason this bear loves to eat more ants during summer. Do you know why? Research and find out!)

-Artic Foxes loves to change their clothes. (During Summer Artic foxes have a darker coat. What are they doing? Don't know? Then research and find out!)

-Water Holding Frogs get down and dirty in the mud. (In Summer, these frogs dig three feet underground. What's the muddy idea? Start digging and find the answer!)

-Macaroni Penguins get romantic and travel back home. It's called a summer-long date night. Ask your parents or a guardian to help you research how long it takes the Penguin to find its way home!

- Lava lizards pack their bags and head to beach. What are they looking for? There is only one way to find out!

I am sure you have other great ideas but these will help you get started.

Something else to think of!

Think of show and tell at school or another school project. Can you talk about summer activities and share with your teacher and classmates? Maybe you can tell them why you like it so much and what makes it different from other seasons!

A nature walk is another great choice. On your walk, why don't you find summer plants and how they handle the summer heat? Can you see butterflies flying around? What about birds? Do you hear new sounds you haven't heard before?

Just one more!

Become a science journalist and find out how some animals adapt to extreme heat.

Think of the Sahara Desert. A cute little animal called a Jerboa doesn't have to drink water to survive. How is that possible? This might be a great science project.

If you choose a desert animal as a science project, don't forget what you need to do.

You will need to do five things for your Science Project:

1 – You need to ask a question to be answered by observation or experimentation. Make it a very interesting question so your classmates and teachers will be excited to learn the answer!

2 – The next step is to state a Hypothesis. This is a big word but Sciencekidsathome.com explains it like this: *It is a tentative explanation for an observation, phenomenon, or scientific problem that can be tested by further investigation.*

So your hypothesis is what you think the results of your project will be when your research is all done!

3 – Next thing to think about is Procedure. This is very important. Procedure will help you to find the answer to your question and prove what you are trying to say.

4 – Results. You will need to show your results and all the information you collected for your project.

5 – Conclusion. Finish up with what you learned and then answer the question you had in Step 1. If you are unable to answer the question, this is also a great place to put the reasons why the question cannot be answered.

(Source: _www.randroades.wcpss.net_)

I know you will have fun learning about summer time! And there are a lot more you can still learn if you just take the time and do it. If you don't like the ideas in this book, put on your thinking cap and come up with your own conclusions!

I am sure you will do an amazing job! We hope you have enjoyed this book on Beautiful Summer but always remember…

"Educating the mind without educating the heart is no education at all." - *Aristotle*

Happy Learning!

Author Bio

K. Bennett loves to write for both children and adults. Many different subjects are interesting to develop, but writing for children is special to her heart.

Her favorite pastimes include reading, traveling and discovering new things. Each of these activities helps to fuel her imagination and acts like a blank canvas waiting for more stories.

She is intrigued with fantasy elements like hidden worlds and faraway lands. And basically anything that gets her imagination soaring to new heights!

Her writing credits include children books online, short stories for online magazines, and novellas listed at Amazon.com

Our books are available at

1. Amazon.com

2. Barnes and Noble

3. Itunes

4. Kobo

5. Smashwords

6. Google Play Books

Download Free Books!
http://MendonCottageBooks.com

Publisher

JD-Biz Corp

P O Box 374

Mendon, Utah 84325

http://www.jd-biz.com/

www.ingramcontent.com/pod-product-compliance
Lightning Source LLC
Chambersburg PA
CBHW050847290526
45792CB00002B/560